Kingdom Of Grace & Romance

A Book of Poetry

By

Ricky Hayes

ID: 4743939
ISBN-13: 978-1497533707
Copyright © 2014 Ricky Hayes
All rights reserved.

Table of Contents:

Introduction

Light Of Faith	1
Serenity	5
Awake The Living	9
For The Sake Of Love	11
Shroud Withdrawn	13
Encounter	15
Think Or Believe	17
Our Hearts' Reply	20
God's Imagination	23
In Your First Breath	27
Grace Child	29
Depths Of Grace	31
Meadows In The Sky	33
Love Is Forever	35
Unbound	38
Intimate God	41
Hidden Away	42
Night Without Darkness	44
Everlasting Love	47
Inside Your Grace	48
Jesus	49
Above And Beneath	51
Choosing To See	53
Beat Of Your Heart	57
All Days	58
His Whisper Is A Lion's Roar	60
Light Upon The Rose	64
Accolade	66
Kingdom Of Grace & Romance	69
Invincible Glory	74
The Lion Speaks	77
Nothing More	79

Harmonizing Truth And Grace	84
Returning To The Truth	87
The Drawn Line	89
Love's Declaration	92
One Voice	95
One Nation Under God	97
A Drunken Soul With A Hard Truth	99
Brighter Than The Sun	105
Reconciliation	108
Signs	111
Fire	114
Joy Above And Beyond	116
When My Lover Is With Me	119
Equal	121
Dare	123
A Perspective Of Beauty	125
The Stallion And The Painted Sky	128
The Wanderer	131

INTRODUCTION

"For by him all things were created: things in heaven and on earth, visible and invisible, whether thrones or powers or rulers or authorities; all things were created by him. He is before all things, and in him all things hold together," (Colossians 1:16-17)

I begin with this because the desire for my life is to truly point to Jesus my savior, who is the Gospel, where in him all things are held together. This being said, God has placed a new boldness in my heart. In a new encounter with him, Christ the one and only, has passionately romanced my heart that I may know the words written in this book and what I have come to know are true beyond what I can begin to understand.

Loved like all of the world (John 3:16), I am held in his embrace, and I have responded to him once again. My first encounter with Christ was when I was seven years old, accepting him as Lord, and my life continued on in a mixture of teachings within the church where I grew up. But the full revelation of the Gospel (Jesus) has finally captivated my soul. What I realized, after feeling called to leave the church I knew my whole life, was that my heart desperately yearned to experience all of God, and find new days of intimacy with him.

Certainly, good people and powerful messages about facing life were preached, just like in many churches or events I attended. Yet the Gospel is not a topical teaching, it's not a theological study, it's not even taking action in a ministry; it's wrestling with Jesus Christ. I realized the reason I was not feeling the intimacy with God I so longed to have was because there were many messages I sat through where Jesus' name was never even mentioned. I was hearing sound wisdom, yes, but my soul longed to hear about Jesus and who I am in him. What does Jesus think about me? Who am I as a child of God? What am I?

These questions and many others didn't get answered until I left and began to wrestle with my savior. I began to see many similarities in other churches by visiting, watching videos online, and reading articles. I realized that many congregations seem to fail in four major areas.

First, talking and helping people visualize intimacy with God. I am not referring to smaller groups who meet outside of Sunday Morning. I am referring to when many are gathered together. There's a routine of protocol where instead of gathering together and sharing the Gospel, we simply listen to topical teachings, extensive theological studies, practical wisdom messages; then we wonder why people struggle or become stagnant in their faith. I believe simplicity of the Gospel needs to be revisited and remain, which is simply getting to know our savior, his love and who we are in him, his finished works.

Second, begins with what a wise women once told me. If we surround ourselves with people who are very similar to us, then we don't really ever grow. So my question is, where are the Charismatic's in the conservative congregations and vice versa. I also heard a wise man once say if there are two people, one sitting in a chair enjoying God's presence and the other is rolling around on the floor laughing their head off; they both judge one another because both of them feel the other is not doing what God wants. I don't remember learning this in Sunday school class where simple things are taught. But when we make things more complex by not speaking the simple truth, these things happen, especially division within the body of Christ.

Example, a man after God's own heart (King David) danced around like a wild man (1 Chronicles 15) when the Arch of the Covenant was being brought to the city. He was covered in blood from sacrificing seven rams and seven bulls. But in a conservative congregation, where is the encouragement to dance before the Lord. Or in the Charismatic church, the same man after God's own heart was laid down beside still waters, (Psalm 23). Where's the encouragement to explore that in the Charismatic congregation? Like I said, we seem to stay with what's comfortable and what we prefer, rather than stepping out into what isn't normal for us. When we step out, we experience growth. But we need encouragement to do so.

Thirdly, we are the body of Christ, and we need to be unified by our differences (1 Corinthians 12), because we were all given one Spirit to drink from. So however you manifest the glory of God who dwells within you, why do so many of us look at something weird to us and say, no, that isn't God. Are we not all held together in Christ? Where is the reminder of our freedom in Christ? Is God just discipline, or is he also fun? Would we just fall to pieces if we changed up our routine services? I'm not saying we can't plan things out and be done in a timely fashion. God loves order, but I don't believe he loves complacency in our repetitive Sunday mornings, or the fact that we're so concerned about our time. When we're gathered together as the body of Christ, we're on his time, not our time.

Lastly, the exploration of who God is and who we are in him. So many times I feel what is preached is safe. We look at all the numbers we're building up and keep the theme of the messages going instead of pushing the envelope and exploring who we are in Christ. Even in a huge congregation, we can get the hamster turning in people's minds to go further. We do extensive Bible studies outside the congregation, but I can't count how many Christians I've run into who believe they're still sinners.

How can light and dark coexist? (2 Corinthians 6:15-18). I remember hearing people talking about the fact we are still sinners for so long that in my emotional state at the time; I actually started to believe them. Thank you Jesus for bringing me back to the truth! I believe we need to have people take responsibility to remind the congregation about who we are in Christ and what his love looks like.

What else can we say that will offend us. How about (Ephesians 2: 6), "And God raised us up with Christ and seated us with him in the heavenly realms in Christ Jesus." It doesn't say we're with him only in spirit, we are there in his eyes! Yet this doesn't get talked about, and so many Christians don't live out their lives as if they are already seated with Christ in heaven. It's a constant toil believing that one day when we die we'll be in heaven with Christ. Since when did death become our salvation? I thought Jesus was supposed to be the only way. If Jesus didn't save all of us, as in he just redeemed our spirit; then that would be like God giving his children one third of a toy and telling them we'll get the rest after we die. What an evil God! Fortunately the truth in Christ is, we are no longer sinners in his grace. We no longer have that label.

Also, in wrestling with Jesus; I have come across the argument that if Christians preached absolute grace, it gives people the license to sin. Obviously, anyone who thinks that grace gives them the license to sin needs to go back and read Hebrews 10, specifically starting in verse 26. So we can throw out that argument.

I have received many weird looks for being more Charismatic now, whatever that means. The term actually means alluring, magnetic, or captivating. Apparently, the term that is supposed to mean exposure to God's love is only used to describe the fact that I'm into weird stuff like prophesying, tongues, the weird things talked about in the Bible.

If you're offended already, it's just because I wanted to prepare you for what you are about to read. The Gospel points to Jesus, and who Jesus has made us to be because we are already in him and the Gospel is Jesus. We are in him as much as he is already in us. This is no ordinary book of poetry. Quite frankly, I'm tired of Christians going without hearing the Gospel. This is quite frankly the reason why 40 to 50 percent of our youth leave their faith after graduating high school. After being a youth leader for nine years, I'd say this statistic is a generous percentage, (Read More about Sticky Faith in the Christian Century at christiancentury.org). But the reason is because they don't know who they are in Jesus or they don't know him at all.

In no way am I pointing out things that many haven't struggled with. I wish to remain humble about my own faults, and no I don't know everything. I just know that I want more than what is comfortable and safe. I want all of God. Grace, I believe is a learning experience. But how can we learn if we don't step out and dream about God's love. God gave us imaginations. Why don't we use them to connect intimately with him?

My first book of poetry "Where Dreams Survive" showed my struggle to find intimacy with God. Surprise! God met me and made me aware of his outpouring in me. This book, "Kingdom of Grace and Romance," I hope will utterly obliterate your heart with the same love poured out from Christ that wrecked my own. This book, explores the depths of God's heart where I have the utter freedom to be wrong because I know God gives grace to my soul like no one else can.

In this book are declarations, prophetic words/visions, and truths that even offended myself until I realized God was speaking through me. If you are looking to get a taste of being more intimate with God, then you need to know one thing. This book is not about how to become more intimate with God; it is simply an inspiration to explore it for yourself. Explore the things of God that you usually don't hear about in the church. It is an inspiration to find out who you are in Christ and live out your life the way God sees you. This book belongs to the lover of my soul, Jesus Christ, and it is dedicated to him alone. And yes, I did read my Bible before I wrote these poems. Lord, may we be wonderfully offended...by you. ENJOY!

Light of Faith

Skies grow dark
My soul feels lost in this grand design
Not knowing what purpose I serve

What do I do with this life
My heart wants more
It wonders what else is there

How I long to escape this cage
Of what seems like a wasted life
O' God, how will you romance this spirit

This spirit that is battered and torn
When will you show me your glory
Where prosperity finds my hands

All my life
I have toiled and tried
To be something

Then I sat at your feet
While watching death surround me
Listening to your every word

Now I sit in a place unsettling
I want out of all I've ever known
What is this desire that carries me away

My mind goes to where I cannot describe
For what is clear in your sight
Is blurred in my own

O' God
I want more than what I have believed
To move on and live my dreams

Even the ones that were shattered long ago
Speak and breathe into my body
Revealing holy instincts within

Call me to where you want my feet to tread
Be strong and open wide the doors
Of favor unto my life

I wish to leave it all behind and discover
More than what I've seen
A life where my dreams come true

Be glorified in my life O' Lord
Place my sight upon the victory
That is already won on my behalf

Reveal more understandings of your grace
Where all of my soul is wrapped up in you
Hearing the wonderful wisdom from your lips

I will not try to convince you God
But I will simply sit in these ashes
Till you change this life into beauty

I will leave my heart and soul be
Till you come and mend
All of what I cannot

As beautiful as you say I am
As holy as you say I am
As perfect as you say I am

I still cannot move without you
So my soul remains abiding in your spirit
Waiting for you to speak

My heart patiently and faithfully
Waits to hear you speak
Longing for the life I've always wanted

With every deed or forgiven sin I do
I give you glory with a thankful heart
For I am not the God of all creation

I recognize in every breath I take
Your hand formed me and it is you
Who gives me the strength to remain

My heart chooses to rejoice
Though the mountains have
Fallen into the sea

Affirm my significance
Take my life and shape my soul
To know what truth is in your eyes

Though I faultier
I consciously return to who I am
Out of despair and into hope

For it is by faith I live
Beneath my skin and deeper still
I know and feel you move

In my existence O' God
I whole-heartedly rest in you
The strength and glory of my salvation

Humility is my beloved friend
Wisdom is my lover
Faith is the fruit of my hope

All of which are found in you
Blessed be the name of the Lord
For you are good to me

King of grace
Fall on me like rain
Revealing the light of who I am in you

Render the fears haunting me
Burn brighter in my life
That your love comes and overwhelms

Use what I imagine to your glory
Take me over and be in every thought
Clothe my eyes in light from your own

So I may truly see what is before me
That I may know what is true
Never relenting from knowing I am in your love

Your grace abounds like a waterfall
Falling and filling my spirit
Overflowing me with joyful peace

Serenity

A blurred decade behind
Cradles broken passions and
Destroyed dreams
Where hope once stood
A shattered romance bloodies
The halls of my soul
Lost are the days of my youth
Lying in the grave with the one
Who brought me into this world

I've watched you wash the blood
From the halls of my mind
Pick up the shattered remains
Of all I held dear
I even spit and struck your face
Letting my anger take me
You've dwelled in a temple of malice
With a plague of love-sickness
Flogging you in every step

Even now
My patience is nowhere to be found
Days are filled with madness
Where the only thing that pulls me onward
Is the resilient light from your spirit
But I cannot move and I cannot
Release myself out of this place
For if I had not hope
I would be swinging in the breeze

My body would be laid in the ground
The crimson of my frame would be
Pouring out and taking my last breath
Yet death is not my salvation

Nor do I look to it to be released from this
Prison of discontentment
For my heart is spread out on the sea
Floating upon waves of mercy and grace
So I don't mind waiting to be put back together

Again your rains hide me from
The brokenness of this world
I go deep within myself to see your face
Because I know you are there
Holding me in a loving embrace
In this I can remember and discern
My heart is elated and consumed
By the joy of your spirit
Yes, I am content with your grace

All these thoughts of loss
Every emotion that does not
Carry me into your loving arms
Is false and decrepit
No, I am not in a good place
Yet your spirit still fills my lungs
Giving fuel to the light of my life
I sway in the storm
Letting my trust in you build higher

Death has nothing for me
Which is why I have nothing more
To cling to except for
The love of my salvation
Even though the world passes me by
I know my God keeps me alive
For a greater purpose to come
Where I return as humbled as I am
Into a reality that has taught my soul to know

God is more than what is preached
Eternal love is just a whisper away
Redemption is the Lord romancing my heart
Heaven has always been found within
The lover of my soul
And you O' God
Are all that matters in this life and the next
The day approaches
I am waiting and I am prepared

As my innocent lover cried out
Shattered and broken
Impaled through hands and feet
To the criminals' tree
My God, my God why have you forsaken me
So does my heart cry out
For the darkest night is not sinful
But instead, it is humanity
Vulnerable and ready for more revelations of grace

The intimacy of the Lord
Never left my savior stretched out
Just as I know it never leaves me
Yeshua was human and divine
Letting the night come
Because he knew
A greater dawn was breaking
Where grace abounds for all
Who long for love's illuminating glory

Let the shadows not hinder you O' child of wonder
Serenity burns in you like
The core of the blazing sun
I have opened the windows of my soul
Seeing nothing else but the love
That is faithful in sustaining me always

Even when I see no hope remains
Peace and hope forever beat within me
Because of you O' God

Awake The Living

Love took me
To gaze upon the King of Heaven
Sitting upon his throne
I breathed in and fell down
At his feet in an overwhelming embrace
A surge of joy and awe
In beholding his beauty

Though I tried, I could not lift my head up
To see his face
Then his voice crashed against me
Like tides against cliffs
I felt the heat of his breath
A fiery comfort warming
The very depths of my spirit

In the intense glow of his glory
He said unto me to open my eyes
I stumbled to my feet to see
Great and elegant thrones
Finely finished and holding precious gems
They were all facing the throne
Of the Most High

The thrones stretched out for miles
When I walked among them
There was no end in sight
Further, I walked away from where the
Most High sat upon his throne
But I sensed that in his presence
Distance ceased to exist

Upon the thrones were bodies
Many still in a state of slumber
As if awaiting the coming of an essence
Still there were many who had
Fallen to their knees from their throne
Casting their crowns down at the feet
Of the Almighty who sang out songs of great joy

You are my children
I heard him sing
You are my children who come and
Feast at my table
You are my children with whom
Share in my glory forever
Come enjoy everything I am

When I awoke
There were shadows
In a moment
The sun peaked over the horizon
I felt hope rush through me
As if I knew nothing else
I breathed in and fell fast asleep

For The Sake Of Love

Then the sun climbed above the horizon
Its light crashed upon the wilds
Plains of sorrow soon bloomed with flora
Praising the luminous beauty among the clouds

Dense forests that were once in gloom
Became pierced by the light of a great star
The trees cried out
Hearing the sounds of the sky
Opening up with pouring rain in sunlight
Quenching their thirst and making them
Lose sight of shameful secrets and inspired
Barren wastelands to surrender their dead

The wastelands gave back lost dreams
For the sake of love
Hope was restored to it and soon
Sands grew into oasis' filled with beauty

All because fear left the land
My glory now beats inside her chest
For the sake of love
When her lips touched mine
The lion heart within me
Shined a light upon her soul
And her spirit finds rest in my arms
She is precious to my existence

For the sake of love
I opened my heart to her
A world filled with beauty
By my will I restored hope unto all

I rained down blood for the soil
To teem with life and receive
All things glorious and wonderful
My kiss brought back
Faith and dreams from the grave
I trek its wilds with laughter in my heart
Like a child that knows only joy
All for the sake of love

Shroud Withdrawn

Return to the moonlight
Guided by the evening star
Wonders shimmer in sight
Transcending soul depart afar

Spirit led back to dreams forgot
Once wasted away in the gloom
But God overlooked them not
Released and returned from the tomb

Shadows call to the glow
Of what now shines among them
Unto the dark bestow
An ever illuminating gem

Great is the nightmare in the wood
Love now standing in its midst
Benevolent and misunderstood
Night transforms to day when kissed

Obliteration once surged from the sun
Moving man forward in dread
From the prison cell undone
Awake, walk the beautiful dead

Alive to speak
Of what descends from the sky
Royal esteemed bow to the meek
Tears dried from every eye

Elegance remains tethered to creation
But hope slips from the soul
A longing to feel elation
Seeking dreams takes its toll

Discourage and downcast heart
Refined by fires of faith within
So revelations of joy can impart
Upon a spirit willing to begin

She comes in like a gentle breeze
As the shroud is withdrawn
Sun falls down in peaceful ease
Every worry fade and gone

Encounter

Pull up the sun and
Shatter the skies with your thunder
Reign down your fire on my heart
Engulf my soul with potent fumes
That enrage my lungs with hope and
Still my spirit within your light

Your voice is inside my head
Building up my bones and framing
My sight on your burning desire
For my beautiful likeness of your image
Comes from all of heaven that is yours to give
And you delivered all of heaven to my heart

Long ago I encountered your love
I stepped out without knowing what it meant
To be a new creation and your child
But you have led me to this place where
Kindness swells up inside me like balloons
Only to be released into the atmosphere

Your fire raises me above the beauty of creation
Setting patience in motion within my soul
For it will be a long time before my feet touch the ground again
War against flesh and bone is revealed to my eyes
It is simply a hallucination of shame
Yet as you hold me, I know my mind is clear

I close my eyes and look upon your face
Wondering what beauty you manifest from your pupils
Turn not away from my own
You must stare deep into my soul and set it ablaze
Raising the flames to soar like angels around you
Praising the pleasure of your beauty and grace

The child that I am climbs you like a mountain
Longing to reach your face
If I should fall
My whole being knows you will catch me
Placing me back upon you to continue my play
Enthralled to be loved by you

Think Or Believe

The love of the Lord
Is the riches of heaven
His priceless sacrifice is the
Crown jewel of my heart

My feet walk upon pedals
Cast in front of me
For the Lord laughs and
Celebrates my life in Him

Worthy is the God of my salvation
His name is Christ Jesus
Who destroyed all fear in my soul
Sin weeps bitterly because of Him

It is chained in fire and ash
Alone and blinded by His glory
O' children of the Most High
Let his love open your eyes

You will see that his sight
Is all that matters
Through the windows of his soul
I am humbled

For he calls me holy and blameless
All my wrongs lay dead
With the one I was and who died with him
Let your minds be released from guilt

The Lord declares
His laws are written on your minds
And rooted in your hearts
Cease from works and see his light

His love is effortless
We are sinners no more
But saints counted as his precious beloved
Awaken and know the truth

Our inheritance is grace and hope
I need not dine on insecurities or fear
My God is strong and fervent in pursuing me
His delight is my heart and the faith he delivers unto it

Nothing I do
Can make me more loved by him
Because I am made perfect by his blood
This is the romance of our merger with his spirit

All things are made beautiful
For the war between us and our flesh
Is over and ended in his death
He is victorious

Giving us strength to laugh at
The lies and downcasts shot
Toward our souls and thoughts
His goodness has eradicated death

My God takes aim at all our troubles
His arrows hit perfect bulls-eyes
Dropping them to the grave
I rejoice and call out his name in

Every storm of life
For His glory is there to consume us
With the light of his beauty
And the joy residing in his rest

Think or not to think
For to think leaves room for doubt
Instead I believe with the belief
That his perfect love has poured into me

Doubt died along with him
Who loves me without ceasing
Thus my thoughts are always
Directed toward the love in his eyes

Upon my throne I
Worship his undying glory
His greatest gift ever to my heart
A love that made a way for me

To enter in his presence without sacrifice
Or by my own hands
O' God
The war is over and I live in peace

Our Hearts' Reply

Your glory and your loving hands
Reach beyond my emotions and my will
Whatever my mind conceives
I know you are there to rejoice or comfort my soul

So I am confident to cry out
In the midst of my heartache
You don't let one of my tears
Touch the floor

Your undying love for me
Rings out in my soul
Even when I cannot hear it
I can feel you move within my essence

My heart is desperate O' God
For change in me and in my surroundings
Come and rest among the city lights
Of where I reside

You are welcome to come and dine
On the joy you pour out upon us
I will not deny you the honor and praise
That you so rightfully deserve

I feel like a tree desperate for the rain
Because the ground has been dry for so long
Gaze upon me with pity and do not relent
In showing me your face

My joy is found in you alone O' King
You are the land of promise
O' God, my God
I have not ceased in being faithful

All my transgressions and sins
Have long been forgotten and died
Within the one I was
Show me God who I am in you

Release the revelations of your heart
For my life to blossom like the meadows
Within my sleeping soul
Awake your promises for me

I know I can come before you God
Because you are good and you are
Good to me
And my words carry many questions

Are you the God I believe in
The mighty savior of my dreams
Will you quench my thirst for your promises
When do these desires become fulfilled to your glory

I cannot bring the rain Lord
So how can I live
Unless you come and drown my life
In your beautiful presence

How glorious is the hope of your love
Will you show it to us all
Do you hear the prayers of my heart
Will you show me my purpose in this place

My spirit is broken and my soul sits in ashes
For my life is not what I wanted it to be
Will you live my faith out for me O' God
Because I cannot take another day

To all these questions
I hear you whisper peace into my trinity
My body and soul rest in you
And my spirit opens to your embrace

Yet I will continue to cry out
That you come and fill the city lights
Let your very presence overwhelm
The atmosphere of my life

Take every negative emotion I hold and
Transform it into a hallelujah to your glory
Knowing that you see me as holy
Your beautiful child

Hear my heart's reply to you O' Lord
The question you ask every nation and tongue
In response
Listen to my voice

Come and show your glory
To my heart and where I dwell
Rain down your intimate grace
Upon those who long for change

Sever the darkness with your love
I am powerless to do so
But in you O' God
The streets inside and outside of my heart
Will reply that you are worthy to be praised

God's Imagination

Flames dance all around my broken body
Yet are fearful to come and kiss my soul
My eyes have no choice but to peer upward
At the light several stories above

Joy invades my heart
Bringing only a smile
Of feeling a beautiful peace
Rush through my mind

Beneath the sorrow and sadness
As it envelopes over me
Like smoke rising upward that I
Do not breathe in

There is only glory from the spirit
Placed here within my chest
Upon my back, I stare up
Through crashed floors

My strength is gone
Unable to believe breath still floods
In and out of my lungs
But only the spirit of the living God

Keeps my soul awake
Dripping water from above
To quench the thirst that runs prevalent in me
Beautiful eyes appear to my own

Belonging to a message giver
She kneels beside me
Whispering lovely words in my ear
Concerning the thoughts of my first love

Her sweet expressions overwhelm
All my dreams to focus
Upon the light above my face
It is so close that it kisses my skin

How I know and hope
I believe my God is here in this place
Picking me up from the ruins
Bringing me back to the arms of the woman

Who longs to see my gaze
Staring intimately
Upon her frame
My heart beats wildly

For our love edifies the romance
You, O' God
Give unto my soul
In every day I wake

Broken or not
Why shall I wish to escape and move
From where your spirit lies
You say come and imagine your beauty

What a failure I am to fathom
The radiance of you and the illuminating glow
Of your wonderful face
We bleed together in this moment

Unbelievable bliss and heartache
The peace of my core does not weep
But rejoices in having so much more than
Anything I ever wanted

All my days
I could be in my wake
Enraged at what I desire
Not coming to pass

Perhaps grow bitter for plans not being met
Yet I already have what my soul
Has always craved
The spirit of the living God

I am the resilient prophet
Laying my destiny upon the back of you God
For I simply do and say what you
Compel and inspire my spirit to express

My Lord over all creation
In all the universe
What place do you not fill O' King of heaven
That will not be reached by your love

Arise O' my passions and strengths
In the name of the blood who bore me
Through one sacrifice and one accord
Wake the light surging through my body

Ignite what I cannot do without you
My soul knows the feeling
Of bones mended from your gentle spirit
And glorious restoration of your grace

You bore me to be your son O' Lord
Convincing my heart of your
Cherished resolve to raise me from the grave
My whole life is found in nothing else

How can it be when you my savior
Breathed all of existence into veracity
Yes, my strength is gone
Because it is only yours that remains in me

By my own strength
I could not worship you fully
So you intervened to bring us
Face-to-face

Into an undeniable union
Perfected within your own flawless trinity
Awaken O' my soul and be aware
The awe of love that abounds in this place

Though ruins lay before my eyes
A love beyond measure dwells within
My flesh and is holding together
All that I am

It moves mountains and keeps hope
Directly in front of me
I need not anxiously look for it
The mirror reflects the beauty of my God

I taste all of His majesty
For in the very place where my savior stood
Where nothing was and he spoke
Commanding the universe that I come and live

As his own child reborn
Upon this place I ask O' God
What do you imagine me to be
Of what I cannot begin to grasp

In Your First Breath

How do I look to you God
Your love is more enticing than sin
For there is no battle within my flesh
But only my forgetful mind
My darkness died with you and
Restored my innocence in your grace

I step away from what ails my soul
Wondering how you will allure my mind
Which is wrapped like vines around you
Entangled in your glory
When meditating upon your goodness
The awareness of your rescue is prevalent

Consciousness of you O' God
Breaks me free from any strike
All things are powerless against me
For you romance my heart to pray
Everything from my identity is found
In you alone and I truly live

Your eyes are upon me now
The shadow that was found in the dark
Caressed and loved out of a hardened shell
Thinking of my heart with a blissful smile
Hanging and dripping in the arms of death
You looked up hanging from my cross and saw me

At once it was over
No more was needed
With your first breath in a new dawn
You breathed light into my bones
Grace into my soul and
Delight into my spirit

In the question of how can you
Entice me to never sin again
My soul sees your love
Finished in me through what
You passionately poured out
And I need not debate in myself anymore

For what has sin ever done for me
But destroy my vision of your beauty
Why hold onto what is false and illusion based
There is no foundation in fear
The foundation of life is found
In you alone God

Guilt and sorrow cannot touch me now
Hate and anger throw their hands up in surrender
The spirits that once were lay dead in the old
All that remains is a memory
Sowing a thankful heart from my chest
Where you reign in me for all my days

Grace Child

I did not hesitate when you called out to me
To the grassy knoll where you stood
A backdrop of stars illuminated
Yet were nothing compared to your beauty
There you spoke life into my veins and
Peace was breathed into my chest
Gravity gently pulled me to the ground
Where you elated my spirit with your words
Your glory spread through me like wildfire and I
Burned brighter than the stars in clear midnight sky

My body celebrates its cleansing
Being made holy by you my soul lover
All indications of death decaying my flesh
Will one day fade back into life
Many remain occupied with their fragile frame
Their illnesses and broken bodies
Yet my heart elates the perfection of my essence
Made new in you my beautiful savior
All that I am is transparent before you God
And your glory is reflected through me

The night becomes dawn
Splashed with dyes from heaven
Glorious is the God who lives in me
My soul releases all I believe to know
Resonating only one conclusion
Your logic is not confined to the minds of the wise
For your spirit is an ambassador
Exhibiting your power and loving nature
It embraces and steals my heart from the
Foolishness of unbelief

Your glory is all around me God
It dwells and elates from within these bones
My state of desperation for you
Is not out of duty or process
But of a thankful and freed heart
To eternally look upon your glory and
Live
Your spirit rescued me and your grace
Shines through me
Overwhelmed and consumed by love

Depths Of Love

Upon the mountains of the world
A gorge illuminates up from the depths
Glowing brighter than the sun
From either side I see many jumpers

I leap from the cliffs of sanity
To see how deep your love goes O' God
My intellect is surrendered unto your wisdom
And many call me insane

You catch my falling dreams
In your ever falling chasm
Filled with your holy light
Where I can always see them fulfilled

I hear your voice asking
Why do my children stand upon the cliffs
Do they not know I will catch them
Why are they afraid to fall forever in love with me

My eyes pity them for a moment
Until I begin feeling the wind in my face
The elation of being free and the peace
Of being wrapped in my savior's arms

For love is a risk of everything we know
It does not bend to the will of men
The heart beats only for a lifetime
Yet death has no hold on love

There is no end to the depths
Of your love O' God
The foundations of the cliffs above
Will soon break apart

But I am safe in your hope
The kingdom of love
Is the light of the world
And your voice is beautiful

Meadows In The Sky

The fires of war are extinguished within my heart
Death runs and hides whenever I open my eyes
Wings carry me into vast meadows
Where joy bounds like deer and the dust of heaven
Rises from the long grass
Sparkling like sapphires consumed in sunshine

Your heart gave up all things O' God
Every ounce of gold and silver you possess
To purchase my existence
I am bound to you and you tell me
Go, run and play
Fly among the heavens and far away from the grave

Every ounce of joy that is within me
Comes from your spirit
That has consumed my being
I am wrapped in a love that many try
To comprehend
Yet you always make them look like fools

I laugh the way you laugh
At their fruitless attempts to explain
How to have faith like a child
O' God
Your wonderful heart takes care of me
As I lay down by your restful springs

No bitterness or malice
Treads in the beauty of your grace
All things are held together by your hands
Even distant sunlight
Sings your praise and worships
The love from your spirit

Now is a time to sing away sadness
Because your joy is peaceful
The worries of this world are pointless
I am loved by the Lord who
Creates all things and knows all things
His bliss is like rain that falls in summer

Its warmth brings life to the hope
Of the child flourishing within my heart
For when I stare at my flesh
I see nothing but a child beloved
By the Father of Lights
A prisoner freed from walls of hate and religion

Meadows are in the sky
Untouched by nightmares
A place where the spirit of worry
Flees and hides its face
There my Father's face beams with joy
To see my arms wrap around him

Take me into your hand my savior
Hold me like a snowflake
Let your mind and heart delight in
Seeing me staring back you
I am yours to love
Laying back in your kingdom already established

Love Is Forever

From the days of my youth and
Through the years of manhood
Whenever I've needed someone to just sit
Next to me and be there
I have usually sat alone

Except I know I was never unaccompanied
For you, the Lord my God
Resonated your presence within me
Dwelling and embracing the depths
Of my heart

You have been like a sweet song
Playing in my head and
Drumming the beat in my chest
The resounding joy in my soul
Remains and sticks like honey to my spirit

I have watched all my dreams die
Bringing anger and rage into my body
My lips cried out for my end
But one day my heart finally heard
You O' God are the only dream I have left

What isn't meaningless in this life
Even the works we do for your glory
Are worthless in comparison to
Dreaming of your love
Yearning to see things like you do

How I know faith without deeds
Is dead
Yet my deeds are dead without
Intimacy with you
So breathe me in

The simplicity of loving you is
Like waiting for the waves of the ocean
To come in and wash over me
You will carry me out and
Drown my heart in your love

I will not struggle as you
Pull me down toward
Your beautiful depths
For you are the air I breathe
And I know no harm shall come to me

No radiant galaxy can compare
To the beauty of your grace O' God
Inspired by your own splendor
I was created and born
With a built in desire for your touch

By your hand alone I am
Lifted high into your embrace
I levitate into realms of glory
Empowered only by your sight
That I may know and believe

The earth is filled with your presence
Your spirit is grateful for me
Yes, you give thanks unto your own hands
That I am beautifully and wonderfully made
I am a celebrated child under your grace

You need not beckon me to worship you
I have seen and tasted your goodness
My heart and my soul will not refuse
Even though I know that you do not
Need my prayers and affections

But you have chosen to
Delight in my very existence
How can I not be joyful
Even when I long for the omega
For I know we will always be together

O' God
I know there is hope
The light at the end of the tunnel
Seems so far from me
Yet I know it is there

I know because you have
Never let me sit alone
You are always faithful and loyal
When my friends are not
Always knowing what I need

Unbound

The light of the sun shines through
Pouring waters from your glory
Refracting the beautiful promises
You have made unto our hearts

My senses awaken to the scent
Of the melodious dreams
Splashing down upon my soul
From the living waters of your spirit

Come alive in the light that beams
Down upon my chest
Let me feel your hand wash away
All my troubles and fears

Stoke the fires of my heart
With heavenly oil from the skies
May it be a delightful sound to you
As if falls upon my flesh

Holy Spirit, come and fill my mind with wonders
Affirmation of your glory dwelling
Deep within the mines of my heart
Where your riches are everlastingly abundant

Your strength is an endless joy O' Lord
Laughing and delighting in this child
Playing out in your rains of mercy
Come awaken the glow of my spirit

Shimmer my essence like the stars
That worship your beauty
For this is all I do
Because I am lost within your affection

I am who you are O' God
In the gusting winds of the storm
My heart knows your voice
And my soul longs to hear more

Conform delectable words from your tongue
That speak hope and love into the
Tunnels of my core
Rooted and tethered to your own

Your arms are like the longing arms of a mother
Awaiting to hold her child for the first time
The joy of your heart elates into explosions of light
When I leap into your embrace

For your spirit outshines any light that
You breathe into existence
How precious is this spec you call your child
I am humbled into trembling in your presence

You are the delight of my heart O' God
The very source of love and I long to fall deeper
Into everything you are
Because of this love you have given me

Not even eternity is long enough
To get to know you God
For you are vast and massive
In wisdom and love

Only you can reveal mysteries unto my soul
The wisdom of men is frail and dead
Even their philosophies of you
Stand flawed and will not last for long

It is because your grace outlasts the ages
Compared to you O' God
All intellect is found wanting
Including my own

Rouse in me wisdom unheard
Understandings of your love not yet believed
Take over every thought in my soul
Where my heart stays pressed against you

My eyes have long since desired to be
Replaced by your own and
In my wake or slumber
This peace overwhelms me

All are beloved and forgiven
Your glory longs to abound in revealing this truth and
The beauty of your spirit among the nations
That all may know the foundation of your endless love

Intimate God

The fires of my spirit delve and burrow
Deep into the foundations of your beauty
Forever I look upon you with such joy
That even if I were to turn my eyes away
My mind would be haunted by your face

The way your muscles bend to form a smile
Elate my heart and I pursue every thought
Painting your mind
Your soul brings me joy for no reason at all
I love the way you speak to me in bold humility

When you are in my arms
I feel deeply moved
As you bury your face to hear my heart
The love I pour into you overflows
Like a raging flood

Release all your troubles upon me
For I am the Lord
Let my words move you to love
And sing out my name
I will make you aware of my presence

Hidden Away

Sorrow has refined me to know
What laughter and joy are worth
The wise contemplate death
While fools only desire festivity
Such things bring my soul to
Let go of all my dreams
For there is only one God
A savior without any other way
The very purpose as to why my heart beats
Is found in he who brings meaning to all things

Without you, Jesus, my dearest friend
Silver mountains would not be possible
The rocky terrain with high cliffs
Where all my hopes and dreams take refuge
In fortresses built by your hands and held
Safe from this world that loves to destroy
Even from myself O' God
You are not afraid to protect them
For now in this moment I lay beneath
Dark clouds of somber sadness

I can feel your spirit moving through me
Healing the inner dwellings of my heart
My soul knows not why it boils and aches
Nor does my spirit understand the anguish
But I know you are there O' Father
Surfacing memories that
Hinder my intimacy with you
I will sit and be silent
Unfazed by this familiar sensation
A burning black star

What goes on inside this heart of mine
Windows and doors close
The room becomes filled with gloom
Yet a light still burns brightly within me
I am falling apart and yet
My heart still feels you near
It sees your arms holding me tight
Beneath the shadowed mists
You hide me away from what ails my soul

Night Without Darkness

Not one portion of me is unholy
For if there was
Our intimate communion
Could not exist

My words would fall upon deaf ears
Yet your spirit leads me into that place
Where my heart is open
To see myself through your eyes

You have forgotten all my wrongs
Placing your laws in my heart
And engraved them
On my mind

In your glory O' God
My trust has no boundaries
All my fears and insecurities
Melt away in the fires of your embrace

The strength of your love
Pulls the stress out of my body
Replacing it with beautiful joy
I have already entered into your rest

Only your name holds my head up
To look upon your face
You breathe hope into me
It is like a lingering, sweet scented vapor

Even my faith belongs to you
I cannot believe in you without feeling
Your love filling my soul with your spirit
So I will always call upon your name

The elation of your grace
Abounds and increases an ache within me
To know more of your thoughts
More of your unending love

I drown in the depths of your heart
Filling my lungs with peace
The intellect of my mind grows dim
When I look to see what you want me to know

Of this unbreakable love
That is in you
It is a raging storm of beauty
A consuming light

My heart is always open to your presence
Teach me the songs of your spirit
The ones you constantly sing over me
Those songs that lead me to worship you O' God

Fill and swirl the windows of my soul
With your enchanting adoration
For your image surrounds me everyday
Staring back at me from the glass

Mark me with your kindness
For I cling to you
As a branch to the vine
Growing and nourished by you

Taste of me and know
Your love overflows in me
Delight yourself in my existence
Touching my soul with your gentle grace

For all I can think of is
Being in love with you O' God
An ever fulfilling enjoyment of you
That transcends time

Let those with ears to hear
Discern that your love is
Simple and beautiful
A night without darkness

From you all things good flow
Because you are good O' Lord
A God who whispers sweet words
To my essence and sees
Me blameless and utterly pure

Everlasting Love

I'm not the one to send
To show your love
But you send me anyway
For I am always in your heart

My burdens are all broken
Death has been blinded
By the light of your glory
And will never find me

This earth and this flesh are nothing but
A shell containing taste after taste
Of your glorious breath and your
Stunning splendor

You send me out like a hurricane
Among wolves in the dark
They are blown away by your power
Residing within me

None can stand against you O' God
All will shout your name and
Praise your sovereignty in the streets
The day, love revealed everlasting greatness

Inside Your Grace

Let me feel my heart beat inside your grace
Pour confidence into my soul in this place
That you are all around
Open my ears to hear the sound
Of you breathing
Your face in front of me sheathing
My eyes from all things but you
No evil thing shall pass through
The strength of your glorious light
Is my whole life and is found in flight
Through the depths of your heart
This tether linking our chests' is never torn apart

When my soul feels unsure
I will trust you and know I am secure
My heart refuses to let go of your love
It is more peaceful and elegant than a dove
More joyful than a lion resting in the shade
Greater than the foundations of world you made
The essence of who I am is found in you
Your glory always points toward what is true
Raising persistence up in the wasteland of my soul
Great is my peace knowing you are in control
Of the air I breathe in night and day
Inside your grace O' God I will always stay

Jesus

I think so much you O' God
Pondering who I am in you and
Who you are above all creation
My soul forever longs to be close to
Your beauty and know
The touch of your hands

Be lifted high in my life
I remain confident and humble in you
Knowing you are good and indescribable
My soul searches to find the words
To praise your greatness
Yet is drawn to silence

Holy, holy, holy are you O' King
A splendorous desire you are
Held tightly in my heart
How can I refuse your beautiful presence
You are my destiny O' wonderful God
Here I respond to you with the love you gave me

I have placed my fingers in your hands and feet
Placed my hand in your pierced side
But I believe in you because your love is so clear
Revealed to my eyes by the grace of your spirit
My heart knows nothing apart from you O' God
All my desperation for you brings joy and peace to my soul

For I cannot stop thinking of you
Your blood has anointed my head to be your child
A king who worships the Father of Lights
You, Jesus, are my one and only
A cornerstone of bliss and
Rest for my existence

All my days I will wander your glory
Even in the days of eternal life
From glory to glory I stand in your light
Enjoying the pleasure of your face
Feeling your love run through my veins
Bringing me to my knees to worship you

Above And Beneath

Your voice calls me by many names
Each one you have given unto me when
Truth blooms in my heart
When you reveal the possibilities of your
Unending power
Deeply rooted in my reality
Your peace blows a calming stream
Through my soul

You prophesy over my life
Building me up into a fortress of light
For all the world to see how glorious
And how wonderful your love is

I am made and strengthened by your hands
So I bask in the glory of your sacrifice
Courage clings to me like the marrow
Buried in my bones

Let it run deeper than my spirit
For only in you do I find
All things
Now they are found
Yet I am not satisfied
Your love stands before me like
A wide open ocean
Waiting to be explored

With endless depths
I need not worry
You are the air I breathe
Your love gives me life as I dive

Swimming effortlessly
Empowered by your strength alone
Above and beneath
Light crashes into me

Your love is open to me like
A wide open sky
Waiting for me to fly into the warmth
Of your arms
Even though they are always
Wrapped around me
For joy and peace find my heart
Without any toil or trial

Choosing To See

My imagination is wild
So I've been told
As if such a thing is undignified
Why wouldn't the God of my salvation
Be beyond my wildest dreams
How can it be that the one to show
The full extent of his love
Through outstretched arms
Would not overwhelm my soul

He is glorious and he has captured
The praises of my mouth and
Thankfulness of my pounding heart
In this chest consumed by His greatness
All I know is that salvation is not a place
Nor is it a process of being redeemed
But in him who took my heart
Within himself
A single moment, he took it all

Together and bound in his sacrifice
He made it possible for us to die together
Redemption is he who resurrected me
To romance my heart forever
I become aware of his goodness in
The realm called the mortal plain
Never to die again
Yet to breathe my last breath and return
To the very thing where God formed us all

No wonder those who turn to you O' God
Have peace beyond imagining
For instead of falling into the grave
We return our shell to where it was formed

Leaving mortality behind in one moment
Just as in one moment you freed me
From the bonds of my torment
The sinful man and his nature are gone
Like dust blown away by the winds

I choose to see your glory because you
Revealed it to me O' beloved Father
My imagination is held by your love
And when my eternal reality comes
It will be greater than I ever fathomed
Because your goodness is far beyond
What I can believe
You are in my dreams and you haunt me
With beauty that I crave in wake or slumber

Take me deeper into your wonderful heart
Place my ear upon your chest to listen to
The dreams of your spirit
I don't need to understand nor do I need to
Figure out scriptures to experience you
There are untold wonders of your grace
Yet your word will always remain my most
Precious truth and the sweetest scent
For your word is breath from you and alive

Your presence is like a
Torrential rain
Heavy upon my soul
You strike me fiercely with your passion
It is a thunderous love
Washing away all my fears
Pride sinks to the depths
Of the waters deep
Never to be reclaimed

Like an owl in the night
You called to me to come be
Beneath your wings and
Carried away into the beauty
That stretches across your kingdom
Your talons lay me gently in fields
Of glowing lights and I wander in awe
Fully embraced by your spirit
I walk unharmed through the dark wood

When my heart reaches the sea
It crashes and pounds against my rock
The God of my salvation
He will not be moved and I stand upon his
Undeniable glory and power
He has built a fortress for my soul
Among the storms of the earth
I have no fear in the midst of chaos
For my existence rests in him

Do not dissuade me from my path
I cannot let go of the God
Who passionately pursues my heart
Even after he has won me over
He is the author of definitive peace and joy
His kindness spreads out among the nations
Calling them to open their eyes
Never relenting to delight in
Every breath they take

This I have longed to see
My God is greater than what I know
He is the light on the mountain I climb
For I know the taste of his love
Is worth the risk
His strength keeps me from

Falling to my doom
And when I slip
He simply gives me wings to fly

Your love for me O' Lord
Pierces my chest with the unknown
My lungs breathe in glorious mysterious
The holy light running through your veins
Is the same that runs through my own
O' God, I am consumed by your spirit
And you need no one to defend your goodness
For you make it known like the falling rains
Breathe on me and reveal more of your beauty

Beat Of Your Heart

There is a thunderstorm
Beating inside your chest
It puts my mind at ease and
Puts my heart at rest

I am safe in your cataclysm
I am loved
I am accepted
I have been made perfect

My ear is pressed against you
You who are my savior and
You're the only one who remains
Wholly to my soul

You hold me fast in your cataclysm
You are love
You are revelation
You have made me perfect

All Days

The works of your hands
Are burdened in ease
For your love
Runs steadily like a peaceful river

Through my veins
It is a beautiful message
Of your grace
For I fear nothing else

When I come into your presence and tremble
I am overwhelmed and frightened
At how great your love is for me
But I do not run and I do not dread

Your hand is upon my chest
Keeping my heart beating and my lungs
Filled with the very air I breathe
You the source of which all life flows

Every vision you bring to my mind
Is a picture of how much you love me
Or how you wish me to see those who are unaware
Of this unbelievable love

Your unharnessed passion that has brought joy
Unto a world that hates you
Is what I have chosen to see and hear
The truth beyond the veil of mortality

I do not understand this grace
Which has saved me from the shadow of death
But I am certain of its faithfulness
Because all my hope takes refuge in you O' God

You are my holy delight
My everlasting comfort and joy
The kind words from your mouth
Speak light into my soul
All the days of my life

His Whisper Is A Lion's Roar

Day and night
My soul and my spirit meditate
On your law O' Lord
The law of salvation that is only found
In your finished blood sacrifice

You do not take pleasure in discipline
Nor in works of my own accord
But you delight in those who come
Unto you for intimacy and hope
You lead them into revelations of your glory

In all my wondrous deeds O' God
Your name is lifted higher and higher
I sing your praises in my graceful compliance
Of your will and your commands
For by your blood I am your child

Every day of my life
You hold me close to your heart
As you sit upon your throne
I am carried in your arms
To the table of your glory

When my eyes close to slumber
I long to dream of your wonderful spirit
The love that is everlasting and the love that
Possesses my being
My heart is compelled by your beauty

I am drawn to look upon the people of the world
Through your gracious sight
Even though I may be just a spec
You hold me in your hands like a precious jewel
Hiding me from thieves who would take me away

I shine like the sun to a world of misery and hate
Those who share intimacy with you O' Lord
Are beacons shimmering with joy and peace
Our thankful hearts draw your light to the darkest places
Because I am beautiful and holy

For this is how you see me God
As I dwell in your most holy place
I think only your thoughts and want only to see
The greatness of your finished sacrifice
All that I am has been redeemed

Though my body is a tent wasting away
On this earth
But you have built me temple to dwell in
Forever in your arms O' God
I sit there upon my throne even now

My ears hear nothing except your voice
The whisper of truth that blows
Through the forests of my soul
Bringing rain to soak me with peace
Erupt my existence with your joy O' God

The glory that shines down upon me
I can feel it always
No matter what my circumstances are
My heart runs through fields of delectable crops
Eating and drinking beyond satisfaction

For I am confident of this
Your goodness I will see
In the land of the living
Death cannot touch me because
Of your undeniable loving sacrifice

It is finished and it is over
There is nothing more I must do
Nothing more that I can do in this life
You've put your law in my heart and have
Etched it on my mind

Only by your blood and death
My Jesus and my Father
Have you laid my fears to rest
You look upon me and see
Nothing wrong with who I am

So I will obey you and I will
Love every moment of you
Embracing my essence
I feel you in my body and my soul
My spirit is intertwined with yours

O' God
I live by your words of love
It is finished
Despite what mockery comes
No, I will not sit in that seat

Nor will I stand in the way of sinners
If those who wish to see themselves as such
Let them dine
In their despair and works until
Truth is revealed unto them

I will not walk in the counsel of the wicked
For my delight is in your blood sacrifice
The reason why I live and breathe
It is by your grace and it is all my hope
My essence is a tree planted by streams of water

The fruit I bear prospers me
So I look to you for rain
Let nothing stand in your way
In keeping your arms wrapped around
My wanting heart

To look upon you my God
As a symbolic teacher is nonsense
It is by you alone that all life flows
I have one more day only because you
Will it to happen

When I leave this world behind
Only by your hand
Will my eyes open to see
Your face smiling back and I will
Worship you in your glory forever

I will embrace you
Desperate and trembling
For you are God
And the passion of your love
Shakes the very foundations of my life

All that I am comes from you
How can I forget the hope you have placed
Within the depths of my heart
Your whisper resounds like a lion's roar
Even to me now

Light Upon The Rose

Your love poured out for me
Is a crimson passion that forms a rose
Becoming a gift unto us all
Such a symbol is a vision of your splendor

Perfection in bloom and planted in my heart
It's thorns are the weakness in my side
For in wake or slumber
I cannot stop feeling you

You are my constant weakness
That brings me great power to see
All that is before my eyes
Uplifting the veil to what you know

Greater revelations of your love
Are found in simple things
Like breathing and feeling
The dawn upon my skin

For my whole life
Is grafted into you
Like the rose that buries
Its roots deep into the soil

The earth is my heart O' God
And your glory fills it
From farthest east to farthest west
My existence flows from your will

All the world is changed
But all eyes are not upon your glory
Yet your faithfulness persists even when
Darkness tries to hide us from you

Beautiful is the weakness to your love
That you have given unto us
Though many let it die or destroy it
In me
It blooms with every dew drop of your grace

Accolade

The five affirmed
Witnesses to your power
Given unto my spirit
A massive weapon of strength
Double edged and easily clasped by my hands
For the Lord trained my heart to wield it

She is called resilience
As it was woman given unto man
To bring strength unto him
Thus my God has given me an angel to
Cut through the darkness
Before I even reach the gloom

Seven years
I kneeled at your feet O' God
Enraptured by your spirit
Though I struggled and fell
You always picked me up to continue
The accolade of my heart

I allowed doubt and grief to blind me
And I bled revulsion out of my body
Hatred beat my soul without mercy
Yet you did not let me break
Then darkness left my eyes
Released from a prison of unaccounted nightmares

From all the agony and despair
The depths of my soul realized
My essence was always romanced by your love
Simple things became clear
You are the air I breathe and my heart
Beats only because you allow it to do so

Then you presented me with this
A weapon I call courage and hope
It is filled with starlight
Cutting through the darkness
Before I even reach the gloom
For you are the source of my strength

Only by your will can I
Hope to wield it and call upon
The beauty of its shimmering light
For it is only in you that I live
All of my existence is found in your sweet
Loving embrace

What am I without you
The beat of your heart took over my own
Your gracious spirit fills my veins
With healing and wisdom
You have made me like a well-spring
That never dries up in the wasteland

Because you believe the best in me O' God
I will not be like the fools who respond
Believing the worst in you as their
Circumstances dictate
My heart will pour out its frustration
To make room for what you pour into me

Death is but a veil
That you have torn asunder
Whom or what shall I fear
Through your eyes I can see
Beyond the curtain and taste the beauty
Of your wondrous spirit

I will not listen to the pastor
Nor the teacher and
Certainly not the ignorant wise man
Who speaks of your love being earned
Every day when I wake
My lungs breathe it in

The holy place has been opened to all
Everyone stands in your presence now
By the power of your grace
Our response to love you is but a nod
To know you, the God that is love
For by your decision do we live and believe

Your heart romances the depths of our existence
Beyond our emotions and intellect
We are simply in the consistent accolade
Of you singing your love over us
Humility suddenly becomes an unbearable longing
To respond and worship you, the living God

Kingdom Of Grace & Romance

You come to me and
Surge strength through my bones
The power of your love
Rouses my feet to move forward
Because fear trembles at the sound
Of your name

Every spirit clears wide
A path for your glory
By any who breathe you in and
All things tremble in your light
For your passionate love
Is beyond any beauty fathomed

I hear you laugh at the darkness
Trying to rise against you
Blissfully I move through the black forests
Empowered by your perfect love
Your glory consuming every particle
Of my essence

On the other side
From the tree line
I see the fires of fear marching
Glee valiantly arms my soul
With hope and faith
For the battle already belongs unto you

O' King of Heaven
You are more than inspiration
Of mercy, hope and wisdom
My heart is grafted into yours
Its melody lunges me into your embrace
This desire of love within me is irrepressible

I watch fear cease
For well springs raise up
Wherever I tread
In you alone do I exist
My spirit will not perish
For you never cease in holding me

All things are open to my life
In this kingdom of grace and romance
Where I rest in your love
To walk among your enemies
Without fear
They fall at my feet

For the victory was yours
O' King of my Heart
Before I could open my eyes and
Before you breathed out
The first star of creation
Now I dine and feast everyday in you

I walk among your vineyards
Vast and teeming with joyous fruit
Every night we drink and feast
As I listen to the stories of how you know me
I was with you at creation
For I was already a memory in your mind

We bask and play in your fields
Unafraid of the dusk
That once brought nightmares
Now it brings overwhelming peace
Where I lay down under the lights of the sky
And walk upon the raging seas, unhindered

All the days of my life
You have lifted me up in your glory
Because you are pleased with
The beat of my heart and every thought
I will not resist in worshiping your eminence
Nor your undying faithfulness

When I was young
Every day I desired to be like you
Then you revealed that from birth
I am holy in your sight
Before I knew you
I was chosen to come embrace your heart

No amount of prayer
Nothing I have done has
Brought me closer to you
As I was conceived
My free will was fused with
Your predestined love

You haven't even blinked during
My lifetime
For you don't want to miss
A moment of watching me live and
Breathe in revelations of your beauty
It is only by your grace that I know now

I have been made holy like you
My bravery is only found in enjoying
Your presence O' King of Joy
I am bold because your love opened the way
To feast at your table
That you carry me to like a king

Kingdom of Grace & Romance

You lead my heart into your romance
The awareness of all things simple and holy
A story of us together as Father and son
In a stunning and perfect union
Your spirit rushes through my veins and
Renews my soul when I grow weary

Even now in this place
Where many dread the coming
Destiny of these tents
I know you have a temple waiting for me
Built by your own hands
Slumbering upon my throne in your care

When I think of your wonders
My soul hears you whisper
To walk this path of grace
I bow down to your goodness
And surrender all I hold dear
For you woo favor unto me

In this kingdom that dwells
Within my existence
A galaxy of dreams shines brighter than
Every star combined
Even those I believe are too wonderful
To fall upon my life and bless me

You make me bold and strong to keep watch
Over all you entrust me to have
Many will know and believe in you
For the narrow path becomes lit
In this age where the spirit of man
Seeks more than religion and enlightenment

Kingdom of Grace & Romance

The intellect of the wise is fading
Children born are crying out
Just like my soul did when I first
Opened my eyes
Yet this was not revealed to me
Until the romance of your kingdom kissed my heart

As it dwells within me and
I let go of the knowledge I acquire
Fear loses its hold on me
Because the joy of your kingdom
Fills my nose with the scent of rain
The aroma of true liberty

That which was has dawned
A resurrection of hope
Falls upon cities whose eyes
Are lost to things of this world
It is a final call to hear what is
To be aware of what is true

Such is your kingdom of grace and romance
A God who died and rose to consistently call
Those he loves immensely beyond the grave
All are welcome to find they are holy
Without toil or sacrifice
No sinner is left, but only saints
A kingdom of love that is already here

Invincible Glory

Your love is worth fighting for
So prepare my heart for rest
Against all odds and lead me onward
In the victory you have already won

Search my soul O' God
Destroy the illusions and nightmares
Coming to oppose your light
Fade them away with a song of love

Fixate my mind upon your face
Your eyes that buckle my knees
The intimate glory that beams forth
From your beautiful smile

Collapse your kindness over me and
Make me a champion in your courts
Where angels open a way for me
As I approach your throne to bow before you

Uncover my eyes to see only what you can
Empower and embrace what I do
You place your hands upon my heart
Strengthening the courage of my spirit

I soak in the majesty of your glory
Sensing your holiness and beauty
Moving inside my own shell
Casting out the consciousness of sin

You heal every muscle in my body
For your good pleasure
No illness shall withstand your perfection
Living inside of me O' God

Give me strength to believe
For my faith is you Yeshua
Radiant like the sun and
Treasured like the depths of my heart

Your glory is invincible
Making me brave beyond measure
My boldness to come before your throne
Only comes from confidence in you

Never again will you allow your body
To be broken and never again
Will you allow your grace to go unnoticed
You are unhindered to love

Even as depression comes over me
My soul is downcast and yet I am not shaken
For you have broken every curse
Within and beyond the barrier of my essence

You have made me an impenetrable fortress
Consumed in your likeness and love
Destiny takes over
Which is held in your faithful hands

The darkness brings rams against my gates
But its spirit is broken in a moment
Fear becomes afraid and flees
Routed, without me lifting a finger

My heart is prepared for faith O' God
For it is always a conscious decision to believe
And you are always faithful to give me
The strength I need to be indestructible

Raise me up in this storm and move
Sorrow has become my joy
Like the night turning to day
Such wonders prove you exist
Proving your glory is invincible

The Lion Speaks

Open the doors of my heart and overflow
The halls of my essence with your love
Come and speak what is true and convey
Who I am O' God

To believe the things you say about me
Credits my heart as righteous and
You have convinced my soul that I am
Innocent and holy

At peace and filled with your joy
I see you moving through my veins
Consuming my awareness of this place
The glory of your spirit captures my gaze

My spirit is clothed in majesty
For you have overwhelmed all that I am
I see nothing but a reflection of beauty in your eyes
As I am embraced by your loving arms

Design dictates definition
I am molded and painted for godliness
From the beginning I was with you
Though I did not know it

My face was just a sweet thought to your soul
When stars were breathed from your mouth
The faces of all whom you love
Were set in motion to receive your faithful heart

By your wondrous sacrifice
You are simply my God and I am your child
No law and no ultimate truth
Need be sought when I'm in you

For my soul only needs to know this one thing
What my heart was made to know all along
I was created to love you
The way you love me

Like a lion without fear
I rest in the presence of my enemies
Upon the savannah of my God
Loved unconditionally under the sun

The lion speaks to me and I hear
You roar out like a thunderstorm
Bringing fear to the oceans' depths
All creation trembles at your feet

For it is surely awe to gaze upon you
The same awe you placed within me
As your spirit asserts passion for my soul
And to anyone else who wishes to listen

The greatness of your love is found
In just being in your presence
Listening to how you dream and wonder
Of revealing your unwavering love to me

Roar in me O' God
For the dawn of my heart is now
I hear it from your spirit
Singing grace over me

Nothing More

Wisdom come and take possession of my lips
Courage dwell and take claim of my hands
All of which are in the one who is my savior

I cling to this love that is found
In you who loves me without ceasing
When my eyes turn to look into yours
My heart feels you fall apart
For you feel your endless love return unto you

Anyone can come and stare deep into your pupils
Seeing the greatness of your intimate glory O' God
Here in this place called my essence

I bow down in reverence and
Take pleasure in your embrace
By your exalted mercy
You have made a place inside this temple
Beneath my flesh

You have burrowed far and beyond my soul
Engulfed my spirit with your presence
I search my heart in silence to gaze upon

The starlight of your grace and you have painted
Sunsets through and through within me
Vast colorations that reflect your beauty
Lay inside my humble heart
And I lay down to sleep in peace

I find relief from my distress in you
O' God
You have set me apart for yourself

Hearing every word uttered from my breath
I point to you alone Jesus
For you bring me to dwell in safety
Though the world shatters and chaos
Envelopes all around my soul

There is more joy in my heart than
Persecution can destroy
My faith in you brings me to laugh uncontrollably

Because your goodness feels like the warmth of the sun
I cannot escape your presence O' God
My soul once made its bed in the depths of hell
Still you came and carried me back to your throne
Holding me till my broken bones healed in your arms

My consciousness of sin dwindles each day
Because my focus is only on you
I drown my troubles in your intoxicating presence

Breathing in the glory of your beautiful face
Your love and faithfulness hold me together
It burns brighter than all the stars in the heavens
Even when I was a shadow in the darkness
You were still there to guide my footsteps back to your love

If there is anything offensive to you within me O' God
Soon it is remedied to break and bow down
Before your friendly smile and the way everlasting

Found only in exploring what I cannot understand
The depths of your love and your unwavering presence
It is a kindness if the righteous strike me
Let the righteous rebuke me
I will not refuse it because it is like oil annointing my head

But I know you God
My prayers are sweeter than incense to you
Lifting up the love you poured out into me

Back to you to be a beautiful and intimate response
When rulers are thrown down from the cliffs and
The wicked learn that my words are well spoken
They will cry out and they will be wicked no more
For your grace fills the earth with your glory

All will know you are sovereign my Jesus
Not from war and conquest and
Certainly not from political determination

But because you are God
The creator who saved us all
From the foundations of the world
Knowing we would fail
You love us without ceasing

Let all who don't believe come and
Believe in the one who died to save the world
Not just those who are in the church

His footsteps leave fire behind to give light
To any who are wanting to find the truth
I was saved before I even believed
In choosing you O' God
My soul found you chose me first long before I wanted you

We all share a special place in your heart
Neither higher or lower than one another
But you reach out and pick us up individually

Saving us from the torturous turmoil we bring to ourselves
Yet you, the Lord my God
Are pleased to see our eyes
Staring back into your own
You want nothing more

For you know in that moment
We will never want to look away
The captivating fires of your love

Possess our hearts to come closer to feel
Your breath upon our face
To hear your heartbeat inside our chest
Wrestle with the mystery of who you are
Long into eternity with joy and peace in our hearts

O' beloved savior, my Jesus, and my God
All my days I could be wrong about you
Yet because I believe and because I long to love you

Grace from your everlasting heart abounds
To consume every part of me
And I know I am with you forever
You give me the confidence to
Share my heart intimately with you

So precious are you to me O' God
Look and see I hide nothing from you
I know of nothing unless you reveal it to my soul

My spirit longs to see myself through your eyes
Piecing together who I am in your glory
Losing sight of the land and settling in the
Vast oceans of your endless love
For you want nothing more from me

My innocence is valid
Because of your sacrifice
I refuse to look away from you O' God

My heart beats to hope in you
As my soul craves to know and see
Your glory reigns in this life
Where the land still belongs to you my King
And the people want nothing more than you

Harmonizing Truth And Grace

Thanksgiving reigns in me
With the peace of God
Who exceeds all understanding
He protects and fends for
My heart and mind

There is much joy in my soul
For the Lord is near and
I am anxious about nothing
The Lord my God hears all I
Petition unto Him
He knows my request before I speak

Take me deeper O' God
Into what it means to fear you
I have forgotten the former things
Seeing now that your hands build up
New things to perceive
You make a way in the desert
Streams run abundant in the wastelands

Upon this narrow road I can taste
The life it brings unto my existence
My eyes cannot see the wide road that
Leads many to destruction
For I have received you and I have believed
In your name
You have born me anew and given me the right
To be called your child

I cast all my anxiety upon you O' God
Because I know you and I know you care for me
You foreknew who I am and you called out
Unto my heart to be conformed to your likeness

I am justified because you called me and I am also glorified
Everything was created by you and for you
In heaven, earth, visible, invisible
Even kingdoms and authorities
Because all things are held together in you

My heart continues to desire you first above all
Because to fear you is the beginning of knowledge
I would be a fool to seek out satisfaction anywhere else
And I know in my weaknesses O' God
Your power is made perfect
Giving me the pleasure to boast gladly in you
All my hope waits patiently upon
Your love that keeps growing within the depths of my heart
Bringing me to discern what is pure and blameless
So I know that my life brings you glory and praise

O' how my soul craves for more
Depth and insight into your love
For I don't just listen to you
My heart loves to do what you say
So merciful are you O' God
In troubled times I seek out
Your mercy and grace within myself
And I find it because it never leaves me
What is more is that I have considered
All things lost unto me as useless that I may
Gain what my heart wanted all along

I am never cast out of your presence
Your holy spirit refuses to leave me
All the days of my life
My soul has desired your presence
Even now my spirit remains crying out
With a thankful heart to see more of your glory
The earth is full of your unfailing love O' God

Because you love righteousness and justice
You heal my wounds with songs of love
Guarding the course of my life
Protecting the way of this faithful child
For loving instructions come from your tongue

Returning To The Truth

Uphold my strength O' God of my salvation
My heart aches and longs for more of your
Endless embrace
Arise the strength in my spirit
Like nothing I have ever known

I hear you calling your children
To accept the forgiveness
The gift of love that was forged
Through blood and water
Washing us to be holy

Heal what I cannot O' God
Transform what is believed
Replace it with the truth of your
Intimate glory and grace
Pour out your hope like wine from heaven

Make the taste of your words
As rich and sweet as
Honey from the wilds
Walk and shine through me
For nothing else pleases me more

Your glory transforms all my tears to joy
All my sorrows are wonderfully blessed
By your loving hands
They become beautiful and precious
Like gems hidden in my heart

O' children of the most high
Refuse your minds' troubles and insecurities
Jump from the cliffs
Away from your anxieties
And into the arms of love

Walk in endless light and peace
Feel what I can feel
The intimate embrace of a realistic God
Look past hypocrisy and abuse
The Lord is none of these things

Return to the one who sings
Over you with laughter
The God of mercy holds you
In high esteem and privilege
Calling you royalty in His kingdom

The God who is Christ the Lord
Enjoys every moment with you
Disgusted by your failures
He is not
His eyes are on your beauty

Unlearn what you call your understanding
For the presence of the Lord
Is upon you and he sees you
He calls you his son or daughter
A new creation intertwined with His DNA

His words arise in all who hear
So let yourself hear what is said
Do not turn your eyes upward
For the Lord is right beside you
Waiting to embrace you in His love

The Drawn Line

My heart is bombarded with your passions
The desires of your spirit takes me over
O' God, my God
You are invited to live among your people
Those who worship you in spirit and truth

I beat my chest for change
Every tear from my eyes moves you
For your sacrifices are of a broken spirit
A broken and contrite heart
These things O' God, you do not despise

Therefore, for all who do not know your grace
For all who believe they fully understand your word
I stand in the most holy place
Where your presence dwells within me
There my spirit speaks mysteries to you

All I can do is feel joy
Day and night as I cry out to you O' Lord
O' God, my God
You have ignited greater cravings
That I cannot ignore

Let the simplicity of your message
Grow into a hunger for intimacy with you
The people of this age long to dine
Upon what they do not know they desire
Unlock the doors to the questions

In these days of my moment in time
Give me a distain for malice and disunity
And a spirit that desires prayer and hope
Reveal the open flood gates of your glory in me
So no one can deny you

My heart declares this be the age that
Teaching from skewed theology dies and
Your people speak only about your wonderful love
Of your grace and your truth
Here the line is drawn

Come war with me says the Lord
If you wish to meet disaster
I take back my people
For my glory alone and to see them
Prosper in a intimate communion with me

I hold the world in my hands
Something you will never understand
My passion for you is tired of seeing
Years of struggles within the gates
Where my sons and daughters dwell

My foolishness makes idiots of the wise
Says the Lord Most High
I am spirit and my people worship me
In spirit and in truth
Come and be at peace with me says the Lord

O' God
Make me bold to push through the haze
Bring the tribes of the west to unite
Under you Father of lights
Light the path and show us your power

I cling to you
Wonderful counselor
Glorify your name through me
Where I touch or speak
And fear flees

Come O' God
Romance every heart
That comes into my presence
My spirit surrenders my faith
Unto your will

In this
Let your holiness shine
Take over me God like I never knew
I am but a tent for your dwelling
A spirit bonded to your perfection

Here the line is drawn O' God
Made by your own hand
I have crossed over to side with you
Lost in your beauty and grace
The war is over for me

Love's Declaration

Have you not seen or have you not heard
The world's cry to see the face of the Lord
My soul dwells desperately in His presence
Awaiting the one I know is
So much more than I can fathom
Thus I do not waste time on what is meaningless

Why do you take so much time O' church
In forming doctrine about the Lord your God
Your days are numbered and your thoughts
Will be overwhelmed in astonishment when you
Close your eyes from this world and open them
Seeing Him in all His glory and splendor

How is it you do not yet know
That the love of God runs deeper
Than vast oceans where darkness
Tries to hide its face from the sun
All things are revealed through him
Yet not all things can or will be understood

Was it Iēsous who called us out of bondage
To form doctrine of his word or did Yeshua
Give his children but one command
A command to love the way he did
Christ Jesus crucified to show
God's endless love for all

Fear not O' children of the most high God
Your thoughts are precious to the Lord
But they are only a taste
Of the feast the Father has laid out
Our souls form images of His
Goodness and greatness

These imaginings are the truth about who God is
When they are formed out of love for
Him and for one another
How can you love Him if not also His children
So why proclaim your ways are right and just
While others are not because you do not understand them

Have you never dreamt about
The lover of your soul
Why then do you display distain
For those who dare to wonder
About more than what is taught
Or seek more intimacy with their maker

Why then do we fight amongst ourselves
When we look to the same deliverer
If love is not the center of your teachings
And if love is not the center of your theology
Then whatever you do is meaningless
You toil under the sun without purpose

Have you not seen or have you not heard
The Lord your God made us all unique
With differences that were not made for division
Instead they are divinely set in His image
Nations look on and you scuff and squabble
Over table scraps under the table of the Almighty God

Love declares the feast is on the table tops
Where the portions are plenty and
No one believes less of someone else
Joy becomes the camaraderie of divergent opinions
Culture ceases to clash as the church body
Looks and sees their savior embodied in one another

Like a python wrapped around its prey
Prejudice is crushed and swallowed
Transforming to communal friendship
Energizing the bonds of love
That should already be in place
O' church, you will rise again to show

All things abundant in the God
Who is the essence of love
You will see that when you step out
Into the world without distracting machines
Or spread thin your vision in doctrine
You'll find love in every moment given unto you

One Voice

When I breathe across the valley
Do the waves of the lake
Resist and rebel against me
Look upon the fowl who float along
Worrying of nothing
Of what they will eat

They respond to my call to flight
Resounding in a countdown all their own
Their wings flap in unison
And they are airborne
Never do they fly without one another

The same is for the lions of prairie
Instinctively, they huddle to form
Families in the midst of the wilds
I know I made man to live together
A commune of harmony and encouragement
My sacrifice was just and upholds

Grace to return to all my children
Far more than what was known before
While you are still in tents in the wilds
Unite under my wings and
Breathe in deep the goodness of my spirit

Do the mountains not speak enough
Of my majesty
Perhaps the stars burning brightly
What about the sun that I placed in the blackness
To keep you alive so you can love
When will my children lift up one voice

Without debating theology and death
My blood is your theology and death is defeated
So why do you boast in what you know
Am I not the God of your salvation
Did I separate my grace into denominations
I am your God and I am love's voice

One Nation Under God

I saw the church burn with the grace of LORD
Looking through His eyes to see His vision
A people thriving in love and hope
Then out of my own breath
My God spoke through me

Forever the LORD God Almighty reigns
Come and discover the goodness of my heart
Cease modifying behavior through discipline
And see lives change through giving grace
The same I extended unto all by my sacrifice

This is a call
Out of the ashes and into
The cleansing rains of my glory
Pray and see for yourself
If I speak to you O' leaders of my church

This is a call
For my love to spread like wildfire
I am taking it into the wilderness
To bring back the lost
The ones I call my children

This is a call
What has happened to you
O' nation under me
You speak my name
Only under your breath

I have shaken you
Yet you do not respond
Therefore another way comes
An unlikely place of resurgence
Will put you to shame

Then you will know
I am the LORD your God
My grace will abound in you
Like ivy and bear the mark
Of hope and love

A Drunken Soul With A Hard Truth

With you forever
Inspired and possessed
By you and inebriated on your love
There is no price I need to pay
In order to receive your great love O' God
For you paid my debt long ago

Once I believed I was indebted to you
Because of the price you paid for my life
Then, while in your intimate glory that
Lays me down to rest and gives me
Each and every breath
A revelation resonated within my soul

So many strive to show you love O' God
When love didn't begin within them
The love you showed for the world upon my cross
Was to cancel my debt
Not pay for my life and keep me bound to
Another thing

You died to bring freedom to my existence
Rose again so I could use my freedom
To know what it means to love
Ascended to your throne so I could
Be intimate and touch the living God
Seeing all of creation inside myself

How great is your love beautiful LORD
Showing and leading me to sacrifice
In the realm of ease and pleasure
For your love is not burdensome and
My heart need not to work in ministering
Because you are the ministry Father

Many forget that the gospel is a person
The gospel is you, my beloved Jesus
It is not a set of rules and disciplines to
Conform our lives
We are set free and must not strive for
Everything we already possess

Christ died for the world
Not just people who decide
They want to go to church
We speak of salvation and the choice
Between heaven and hell
Yet hell is believing you're still in debt

Every curse was broken in he
Who is lovely and grace
If not, then we would all be farmers
Toiling the ground to get our sustenance
We would not have pain relief
For mothers giving birth

I am drunk on my God's love and that is my purpose
So if it seems I am out of my mind
It is for my God because I am enthralled by him
This is grace in he who gives me strength
To know the Father of lights through his blood sacrifice
We are freed from all debts

Not just my spirit is saved
No, all of myself is saved and
Beloved in his glory
Did Christ's sacrifice pay for all of me
Or did it just pay for my spirit and now my soul
Is being redeemed inside of sinful flesh

If this is so, I wish my savior would
Just have stayed in heaven and never come down
What good father buys his son
One third of a toy and tells him
When you die, you'll get the rest
How evil is the Lord if this be the truth

Let me be a goat and be separated from him
But as the good news goes
I am already seated in heaven
Where I gaze upon love itself and his name is
Jesus, my savior, my beautiful God
He is sovereign and he has freed us all

When O' God
Will your people rise up to
Betray and abandon doctrine
Religion spreads like a plague
Without us knowing
Because we do not focus on the simple truth

Love is you
It's not a word and it's not what we do
You are a person Father
And your name holds power
That broke every chain and exploded our hearts
From the inside out with hope and beauty

We work because of your love
It is effortless
If it is not
Then it is religion shoving us to
Love you by our own strength
Through discipline and toil

Many will call me false
Because I love you so much
With the very love you poured out into me
They will ridicule my behavior
As I walk intoxicated in your presence
But it is real beyond measure

It is a simple manifestation
Of how pleasurable it is to be
Consumed by the love that is you
An overwhelming bliss and fearful wonder
My heart practices being in your presence
Drinking in the goodness of your spirit O' God

I read and let my soul
Wander in your glory
Greatly filled with your peace
Blissfully dining upon your joy
No, I cannot go back to being
Conservative and avoiding the weirdness of my Father

No, I will not strike up my emotions
That is work and my Father speaks unto me
I need not work for his glory
For it stirs and dwells within my shell
A tent for my soul and spirit
That are drowning in the pleasurable presence of the Lord

Knowing many will come against me
Claiming I know not your word
I know that I can laugh and be merry
For you have placed your word
In my heart
And carved it upon my soul

How great and happy your people would be O' God
If they came and became drunk on your love
The divorce rate in the church would not appear
Like the ratio in the world
There would actually be separation in who we are
Married couples would make love like there is no tomorrow

They would realize that they are
Bound together in your glory
Pulling enough gold out of one another to
Buy the world a hundred times over
Their eyes would see nothing but what
You see O' God

Addicts would lose their desire
For whatever they seek in this world
Because the drunken presence of the Lord
Is so much stronger and much more exhilarating
Than anything this world has to offer
But instead we push discipline upon them

Our children lose passion for the Lord or worse
They fall away and imprison themselves
In a false reality where the illusion of sin
Consumes their lives in lies and misdirection
It is the wide road that leads to destruction
And many in the church find it as well

We consume ourselves with trying not to commit
The unforgivable sin that is blaspheming the Holy Spirit
But we do this anyway when we refuse to believe
Sin died with Christ at Calvary
You claim to know Jesus, my beautiful savior
The roaring lion in my chest

No, you do not
If you believe in such stupidity
Why are you afraid O' church to offend
Get rid of the goats in your midst
Or perform a miracle in the name of the Lord your God
Turn the goats into sheep by actually preaching the Gospel

We sit and listen without questioning
Without wondering and chewing on God
For far too long, we have drank from the words
Of practical wisdom, feel good stories, bible knowledge
Bowed down in altar calls promising redemption
In the one we have already been redeemed into

Why do you run to your Bible O' church
Do you not have the Holy Spirit to discern this truth
By all means search the living and breathing word
That brings so much pleasure to me
But the word is a person
Not just truthful text on a page

Hope and truth are found in Jesus
The person and the only way to the Father of lights
Because he is also God
Where are our children going O' church
Why are they not seeing pictures of intimacy
With their loving Creator

Many children can recite their favorite Bible verse
Yet know very little about how to define grace
Let the joy of my heart give you a little hint
It's Jesus, talking about Jesus, and focused on Jesus
Sharing our inner thoughts about this lover of our souls
Because Jesus is reality and sin is not

Brighter Than The Sun

When I approached the throne of the Lord
My feet lunged forward to fall at his feet
Yet before I could feel the ground upon my face
His arms reached out and grabbed me
The beauty of his glory held me fast and
I was placed in his chest with his arms wrapped
Tightly around my body

The strength of his heart beat
Made me tremble in his embrace
Before I could speak a word
I heard him cry out his joy
I was silenced by his beautiful words
That he sang over me
It warmed my veins as if fire flowed through them

Our sides began to ache
As our laughter became uncontrollable
The elation of being in each other's arms
Was a wondrous sight that when
Nations looked on
They could not understand
But I am held by love

There were jealous shouts and rage
Against my bond with my savior
What makes you so special
They demanded of me
My answer was simple and true
Why do you think you are not
Is it not clear He loves us all equally

For too many years
I believed wrestling with
Who my Father is
Was prideful and improper
Yet my heart burst forth from
What ailed my soul and
My essence stood to face him

I longed to know his face
My heart pounded against my spirit
Like storm tides against the cliffs
Come down I cried out and show me
The goodness of your heart
Awaken me from nightmares
Into a love that I know is real

My soul was ready to burn in the abyss forever
If I was too bold or what if I were to become cursed
How could I believe such things
What bewitched my soul to have so much fear
Then when the light of his grace appeared
Resounding the triumph of him over all things
I knew I was free to express all of myself to him

To come and wrestle with who Jesus is
And fight in his ring of glory
Not for the sake of gaining power or fame
But to get close to him and discover
His strength, his mercy, his love
The greatness of who he made me to be
In him who will never cast me out of his sight

He is the breath in my lungs and the wind
Blowing through my soul
I have become so aware of his presence
My very existence becomes hopelessly lost

Within his beauty and his intimate adoration
Of who I am in him
To deny such a thing would be to spit on his blood

I am holy and blameless
Held high above the angels singing praise to his name
My heart is held so close to his own
Where I cannot help but reach out and touch his face
Wanting nothing more
Than to stare into his pupils
For I am his loving child under his care

What son doesn't want to look in his Father's eyes and be
Everything his Father is
His Father who owns and knows all things
A Father who is greater than any gift given to me
I dwell in the heavens with him even now
With joy and freedom in this life and the next
In my Father who disperses all shadows and nightmares

I shine brighter than the sun
Anchored in the one who shines upon me
The love of you O' God, my Jesus
Is zealous to bring my heart to know
The real me and the love of a holy bond
You are with me as my soul prays all day and night
Because I cannot stop thinking of you

Reconciliation

In the hope I take in Christ my Lord
What is plain to God about who we are
My soul yearns for it to be simple to our conscience
His love compels my heart to speak
The revelation of Christ, the gospel
A stirring fire of faith
Both living and breathing within us all

I am convinced that one died for all and
Therefore all died with him
Those who now live, no longer must live for themselves
But for Christ who died for all
Even you who don't believe are included in
The resurrection of Christ who so loved the world
Awaken from your misconceptions of Jesus

See plainly the way God sees your essence
I speak plainly as an ambassador of Christ's love
You are the righteousness of God
Without toil or effort
By his blood you are his beloved child
Choose to be reconciled and experience
The wonders of your Father's grace

Why do you refuse
Will you allow lies to rule over you
Do you harden your hearts because
Your soul loves evil and to what end
Are you satisfied O' you who don't believe
In the God who believes in you
The King of Heaven who holds you in high esteem

For Christ did not die for the church
It was by grace he died and it is by grace
All are saved and reconciled to him
To deny it and not explore his soul
Breeds destruction within yourself
Let not your appalling experience with religion
Be the example of him who loves you to no end

He wakes you from your sleep
With loving arms wrapped around you
Though life has cut you to pieces
Your God waits for you to come and feel
The glory of his blissful presence
That the joy of your heart
May be complete

I thank all who swear that I am
Out of my mind
For it is for Christ and this unbelievable love
He has placed within me
Whether in dream or wake
My soul devours his endless goodness
A feast of satisfaction for me

Where is the glory of the Lord in you O' church
Did my savior not say we would
Do greater things than he
Because he goes to be with the Father
I cannot do such things without you
No, we cannot stand apart from one another
Like clans competing and warring

Why do you O' leaders repent
For things you have not done
Is God not good enough
That he will not see your own desperation

To come and show his glory today
Awaken into the intimate glory of the Father
Who has already rescued his children

Have you not experienced
Do you not know
My Father and yours
Drinks us in and is filled with unspeakable joy
Because of this
Our single desire is to gaze upon his beauty
While resting in the beat of his heart

He fills the place where you dwell even now
Stirring up his glory within you
See, you were reconciled to him
From the foundations of the world
His sacrifice has brought an unbelievable love
Into you and it will never leave
He even gives you the strength to believe it

Signs

Hate fortifies walls against God
Making you an enemy to be crushed
Under his feet as he steps out in his love
So be careful what signs you hold up

Claiming what God hates
How is it you don't get it
Love is what conquered all things
Not your delusions of God's mind

For God so loved the world that
He gave Jesus to give grace to "fags"
Those who have abortions have grace as well
Even those who don't believe in God

Though my heart desires love and righteousness
I can see them as beloved children and tell them
Who they truly are in Christ even if
They never believe me

In the same way you judge others
You will be judged and
With the measure you use
It will be measured to you

Do you not fear God O' Christians of signs
In the power of his love
Our mighty God who can destroy both
Soul and body in hell

Perhaps you should read your own signs
It's like a spotlight telling God your heart has no love
What little hope you have
You Christians who still believe you are sinners

Though Christ died to finish his good work in you
To give you all you need for life and godliness
You are already living in hell
And you bring your children along for the ride

Grow your little ones up in hate
Then they will grow to hate you
By this
I am boldly compelled to cry out

Grace to you who are ignorant to quote one verse and
Create a way of life around it
Are you terrified to try love
What are you afraid of finding

When did you begin to believe
Or who bewitched you into thinking
That a relationship with Jesus is a religion
When our savior in fact came to destroy

Every single religion on earth
Religion requires effort on your part
To gain salvation and eternal life
But Christ gives no room for you to boast in your own works

Once I was filled with anger and hatred
Time and again my Father's grace
Broke through the fortified walls in my heart
Until there was nothing left but him

He desolated my heart with his love
Which I gladly say is falling heavy upon you now
As the Lord your God has said through his servant
If you do not have love you have nothing

You who still live under the law of Moses
Living as if you can be saved on your own strength
Jesus never wanted to give the law to his people
As you can remember Jesus said

He and the Father are one
Christ is the word from the beginning to the end
His love breathed life into us
When he made all of creation

Where your hearts' seek justice
The Lord said it is his to avenge
No, we do not have to roll over and allow
Laws we know are wrong to be passed

But we stand on the very foundations of love
In one who is more powerful than us
Yet the signs you hold up in hate
Tell the world you actually don't believe in Jesus Christ

You tell the world you don't believe
In his power or authority over all creation
So what are you, what claim do you have
If you preach you don't actually believe in Jesus

For the sign the Lord holds up is always love
When the day comes for the King of Heaven to return
His sign will descend upon everyone in fiery glory
Where every knee bows and confesses Jesus is Lord over all
Because love is the conquering force over all creation

Fire

Not one word I have ever written here
Has been inspired by my own soul
But the desire of my savior
Who dwells richly within me
It burns like a fire
Where my spirit rejoices
Even when darkness falls

I am surrounded in a dense wild blaze
Consuming the foundation of my life
But I close my eyes and hear his voice
Echoing inside my bones
Call me a liar, but I cannot deny it
His presence envelopes within me
Madly roaring to capture my attention

How can my eyes focus upon evil
When all things around me are consumed
Until there is nothing left but my God
Even my flesh is overtaken and scorched away
Exposing the inner dwelling of who I am
And all I can see is my lover's face
The beautiful glory of him who is all things

Nothing I did made him come to pour out his love
Upon my aching heart
He knew my heart longed for him
Before I ever opened my eyes
How can I be afraid
When the light of his glory burns deep within me
Igniting joy like a volcano erupting into the sky

No wonder nations fear you O' God
Your love is more powerful than quakes or hurricanes
Yet more peaceful than a sluggish river flowing
Far more beautiful are you than
Any time of day or night
This faith burns inside of me because you placed it
Within me through your one and only sacrifice

How great are you my lover
What many perceive as destruction
You have revealed to me as passion
A Father's love without limitations
I come to you and fall asleep on your knees
Like a child tired and weary
Forgetting what it means to be scared

All my worries are gone
Burned away into ash and sailing
Far from me on the winds of your breath
I know I am terrified what I will find in you
Yet I am addicted to the wonder and beauty
Of who you are O' God
My essence simply explores onward in your glory

Let it be known that
Your love sparks and spews the heat
To awaken souls to see your presence
Fall upon the world like a burning rain
Consuming all in one accord
Of the beautiful and majestic
Fire of the Lord my God

Joy Above And Beyond

Abused by this life
Only strengthens my greatest weakness
Yet I know your power is made perfect within it
O' God, you have a heart like no other

Every day I am dying to know you
Joyfully moving into your eternal glory
Away from this mortal plain and
Far from this tent to be lost to the wilds of the earth

My soul is very distraught
Seeing everyone around me with all my dreams
Loved and bonded to one another
Creating beauty and living out my desires

I will not lie nor will I pretend
My bones want to return to the dust
And my mind wanders to thoughts of longing
To seek your tangible presence

I have tried to remove myself
From my own head
But the bitter storm rages on
Hoping my next lover wants me

In the same way you want me O' God
For you are the cure to all loneliness and
You've always wanted me for who I am
Not for selfish gain

Here is an outpouring of my heart
I close my eyes in disbelief
That I can still see my reflection in the mirror
Wondering why I am still here

Many would say you have more important matters
Like taking care of orphans and starvation
Around the world
Why would you listen to my troubles

Yet here are all my cares poured out like blood
Flowing from open wounds
Covered from head to toe in my life
I feel your spirit O' God

Endlessly flowing through me
Despite whatever precious hope is lost from my soul
There is no omega to your joy and peace
As an endless river, I gush forth beauty day after day

I can already hear them say
Where is your kingdom of grace and romance
With your so called intimate God
Then they are silenced for my ears pour out

And all I can hear is rushing, living water
Of Jesus who saved me
Bliss becomes my doom
A destiny filled with starlight

My words are the mighty sword dubbed resilience
Swinging effortlessly to cut through the dark
Uncloaking the veil of the ignorant and
The souls longing to feel the truth

Soar through their bodies
For those who long to hold their savior's hand
Reach down to your chest
Because his arms are always wrapped around us

His mercies are new every day
There is never any distance between
The lover of my soul and my flesh
He dwells within me

His hands have has tethered our hearts together
Grafting all of who I am in him
The words he speaks to me
Never cease to romance my heart

Now let the devil come if he can
How terrified he is of this light
Blazing with the beauty of my God
Here in my chest

I will be still and silent
My eyes open to stare into the heavens
That are always open to me
For the Lord sees me in his kingdom beyond this realm

When My Lover Is With Me

Perhaps my lover is there
Among the lilies of the valley
Prancing like a firefly
In a midnight meadow

Or perhaps by the oak that sits
Lonely upon the mountaintop
Ever listening to my every word
Though I lay in my bed from afar

While everyone drowns their sorrows
My eyes are ever vigilant and hopeful
Knowing the dawn is breaking
There she will stand in all her radiance

Like wisdom feeding me
Sweet nectar unto my soul
I will be addicted to her beauty
Her every whim and smile

She binds me to her free spirit
I feel my feet leave this world behind
Before I was living
Now I live in flight

Her endless affection of my soul
Creates renewed strength in me to shatter
Giants of the land and destroy
Any darkness that lingers at my back

Yes, she holds me in a trance
But not of her appearance
It is the kindness of her spirit
That makes my knees buckle

Her beauty overwhelms me in a moment
This is her strength and
My heart guards every bit of her essence
Because she is the light of the dawn

Equal

Winds of her inebriating scent
Blow through the halls of my heart
I walk there among the rolling hills
Shaded in green and gold
In the brisk morn

All day I wait for
Her free spirit to fly back
Into my arms
Night appears and she
Falls fast asleep in my embrace

Shower me with romance
O' lover of my soul
I long and wait upon you to bring
The beauty of her smile
To meet my lips

When will you allow these hands to show
Your love to a pleasurable face
How long till she comes away with me
Into the gardens of life
Blooming with your glorious wonders

I listen to you breathing
O' wonderful savior
Then my mind wanders and aches
Always in the same direction as before
For only something you can give my heart

This desire is so strong that I
Dine and feast at your table
Still in full enjoyment of your love
Yet still wishing to pour it out
Into my equal

I hear you speak of her to me
As if she is already in front of my eyes
But these thoughts are a mist
Settling in my dreams and then
Evaporating at first light

So I hold fast to hope in you
Visions of her pupils sing to my soul
They are like gravity
Pulling me inward to meet her embrace
Hearing her adoring words of affection

Because you have given her to me O' God
I rise and call myself beloved
More than any other son in your kingdom
Her spirit is a gift
Inspiring freedom

Sensing your presence in her
Makes my heart passionate to
Open wide the gates of time
Forever pouring out this love
You have given me

This love is effortless and
It is so easy to adore her because
You dwell within her like you do
In my heart O' God
So do I ask you bring her in as well

Dare

Every muscle I have is rendered useless
When her beauty slams into me
The trees in my heart change their leaves
Into seasonal colorations of fall
And throw them down before her
Like rose pedals for her feet to never be soiled
By the dusty path

The swift kiss she places upon my lips
Drives my soul into a dream
Where I hear my spirit cry out
Hoping that it will never end
She has entangled me in her innocence
Every part of her is warm and sweet
As the dawn and the earth collide

Her touch on my face melts
All the winters I endure
She is the renewing spring of my heart
Bringing winds and rains of
Unspeakable beauty and grace
I see her and I see nothing but life
Then I break apart

Every shard that shatters in front of her
Yearns to reflect her undying loveliness
The blush of her face radiates humility
It just makes my eyes eager to see
More of her wonderful presence
Full of smiles and giggles
She wraps her arms around my frame

This love she pours out into me
Alongside the stars at night
Reminds me of her being a memory
Inside my mind
Even before I met her
Now she walks upon the waters of my cares
Calming any storm that stirs my peace

Her words draw my attention to
Glory and hope
She carries strength to place me back
Upon my thunderous steed
When I cannot stand
And she nurses my broken bones
Waiting patiently for heaven to heal me

She is invaluable
Loving all that I am without ceasing
Every move she makes strikes me with awe
Of the one who created her
There is not a place in my temple she cannot stay
Pulling me into her embrace
My confusion about love fades away and
I dare to live in holy union with her always

A Perspective Of Beauty

Every sunrise is never the same
But always radiates beauty of the skies
It is always a masterpiece waiting to be
Gazed upon in awe
So it is when I look upon her

I cannot outrun the light
Thus I cannot outrun the wondrous
Splendor of her soul
Her loveliness is always warm
Upon my heart like the sun

When she wraps her arms around me
Joy almost breaks me to my knees
She is the most beautiful woman
In every room she treads
An epiphany of love lingers in her footsteps

She finds peace in the wilds of my heart
Freedom in being bound to my love
For I romance her spirit with patience and
Encourage her words of wisdom to shine
Like stars burning bright

She wears my heart like silk
How precious and priceless I am in her eyes
My elation entices hope within her
And my body embraces every moment
With her as if it is the last time

The challenge of knowing her is easy
For I am consumed by a spirit of love
That simply pours out upon her
Days, months and years are peaceful work
Because I am always lost within her beauty

There is no one else
Not even the inveigle figures
Welcoming my mind to wander
Away from my beautiful lover
No, her beauty goes beyond flesh and fantasy

I can never let go of wanting
To gaze upon her in wonder
She is like the cathedrals of old
Filled with imagination and
Reaching for the clouds

When thunder beats heaven's drums
Her face presses into my chest
And I simply hold her till
The breaking of dawn
For our hearts are one

My soul has no choice but to love
Every element of her
Why would I wish to flee
Peaceful is the slumber of this adoration
This love that flows from my lover

I am flooded with
Songs that I am too overwhelmed to sing
Of the beauty before my eyes
As every man should look upon his bride
This is a perspective of beauty

Before all slips away and
Tomorrow is gone
I draw near to her and make
A promise not comprised in fiction
To love her beauty till my heart breaks
Then, love her even more

The Stallion And The Painted Sky

Reflections in pools of fallen rain
Upon the forgotten prairie
Return to the white stallion
Blessed with new wings to soar

Into the sky he roams
Feeling the fires of his passion become
A place for his soul to dwell among the clouds
There, she is painted in the heavens

Her spirit splashed with glory
Saturated in an exuberant lullaby
His wings are caressed by her fingers
As he twists and turns within her atmosphere

Elation from the stallion shines as brightly as her
Sun kissed soul
Sweet and delicate her clouds shed
Life down upon the land and his heart

Drenched in her embrace
The beat within his chest can bear no more
He lands softly to the ground and
Peers up from the ground

Beneath her stormy gaze awaits
A smile of love
Wanting him for her own
She continues to let her rain fall

Pleasant is the aroma that catches
The stallion's senses
Laying him down beneath her beauty
To bask in hope and wonder

His pupils gaze at her
Seeing nothing but gold and rubies
Amethysts are her eyes and
Garnets are her lips

Sapphires take over as she fades into starlight
Shooting across the night to share her elation
Unto the lover of her heart and spirit
Never once does the stallion look away

Dawn breaks and her spirit again comes alive
Beckoning the stallion to become airborne once more
Again to fly into her beauty
The embrace of her love holds him fast in the skies

His head presses against hers
Longing to stare into her eyes till she fades into the day
Noon comes so quickly
Yet dusk comes swifter than a blink of his eye

She is painted above him again
He cannot help himself and tastes
The majestic love of her heart
As he glides along and caresses her soul

To what end shall the stallion cease
His undying adoration and his grown fondness
Of her beautiful spirit
Painted in the skies twice a day

Two unlikely lovers swim in the deep
Of succulent affection
Lost in the bond of the love that
Placed them together

Beyond their form and thoughts
Both found beauty in the other
Where nothing is more important than
The endless devotion to the hope love creates

In one fell swoop
He fades away with her
Never again to be apart
The stallion and the painted sky

The Wanderer

Established and forever sovereign
I walk with you in your kingdom
Sharing in the glory of your goodness
Your spirit holds me as I wander
The world that is your domain
Evil is gone

By a pool of sparkling waters
Her face I recognize
Her smile and her eyes
Are perfect and mine are the same
As hers from days of old
For my God made them perfect then

Her arms are comforting
Like a mother I once knew
She places joy upon my heart
Feeling the spirit of my God
Resonate from her touch
Then I continue to wander

You lead my feet to a place
Where my eyes look upon
Women dancing in blooming flowers
In a vast meadow
One swings a child around
It is a place of beautiful laughter

There is one I remember
From a distance our eyes meet
My hand raises to wave and I smile
She waves back at me
Still dancing in the embrace of God's
Beauty and elation

The other who ceases from swinging the child
Looks at me and laughs
Relating the fullness of the Father's joy
My heart bursts forth with delight and joins in
I remember them and they remember me
Then I continue to wander

I come to a temple
Housing mountains of scrolls
The love letters that my God wrote
Unto His precious children
My eyes catch a glimpse of one
Reading them aloud day and night

My heart rests beneath the tree that
Stretches miles into the sky
Among many children
I listen to the one
Who I remember as brother
And I still call him by this name

Another is with him
Reading and speaking of her fascination
With God's heart
I remember her love for the soul
My lips speak friendship with her
Then I continue to wander

A ways away from the temple
I recognize another
He makes me laugh as I see him
Slumbering atop a grassy knoll
Basking in the glory of God
My gaze turns upward

His dreams come to life in the clouds
Shaping and coloring them
To glorify the spirit of the sovereign King
Even in his dream state
He opens his eyes to share a smile with me
Then I continue to wander

My eyes soon fixate on the simple structure
Of a beautifully finished cabin
Next to it stands a brewery that brings joy
To my heart
For I soon remember the man who comes out
To meet me with a glass held aloft

As I hear the ocean's waves crash nearby
I take the glass from him and drink
Perfected water from the sea
That turns to a fine brewed taste in my mouth
Together we drink and
Feast the night away

With the others I remember
Including the woman next to the brewery
Who's garden is full of herbs and spices
She grows them by worshiping the Lord
And cuisine tastes incredible because
Of the passion God has given her

Another I remember
Who passionately loves and enjoys
The company of God's children
He spreads the beauty of humor
Over everyone and everyone
Calls themselves blessed because he is there

My eyes stare across from me
One that I remember still calls me son
He is covered in sawdust from building
The tables for the feast
There is so much joy beaming from his face
For others I recognize were building with him

Beneath the stars that shine greater than I remember
We feast and dance the night away
The spirit of the living God
Spreads out over us all
Overwhelmed by His glory
We freely celebrate His love and His heart

There are so many I remember
So many I know I love
To love is so effortless now
Because I know and see the eternal end
You make me happy O' God
Then I continue to wander

For in worshiping you
I see a star calling out to me
My heart knows you are there as well
I have to go there
To bask in the wonders of your love
And I remove the ground from my feet

I am drawn toward the light of your glory
Like a moth to a flame
Yet much faster than light can travel
For as I abide in you God
There is no distance
Nothing is out of my reach

I continue to wander
Because it puts me at peace
Every night is a celebration with those
Whom I remember and love
Thus all my affection is tethered to you
O' Father of my heart

My soul and my spirit is drawn to
Romance yours
Beyond what many believe romance is
They do not know now
Yet soon they will
For the time for the end is near

But I will begin now and forever
In the holy union I have with you
My love reaches beyond the stars
As I wander and wonder in
The vastness of your beauty
Be happy O' God knowing I am in love with you

About The Author:

Ricky Hayes was born and raised in Chico, California. He began his studies in the Theatre Arts after graduating high school, but soon found he had a passion for writing. He earned a BA in Journalism from Chico State University and went on to go back to school to learn more about graphic design. While pursuing his dreams, Ricky found he could not simply pass on the obligation to put his dreams on hold and help take care of his mother. She was diagnosed with ALS in December of 2006 and passed away in January of 2009, with Ricky's family also bearing several other deaths dear to their hearts a year before and the year after his mother's passing.

During that time span of seven years, Ricky believes his relationship with God and his passion for writing helped him find a voice in the mass of chaos that he says reshaped his life. He holds true to the belief that in the end, the most valuable pursuit in life is to seek God's heart despite the circumstances because joy and peace are always the core of God's heart toward us all.

Acknowledgements:

I would like to thank God first and foremost for giving me the boldness and the inspiration to share this book with all who are willing to read it. He is the light of my life and the greatest treasure to my heart. I can think of no better way to honor him with the gifts he's given me than to acknowledge his sovereignty over my life and glorify his goodness now.

My thankful heart goes out to David and Mamie Bronson for their hearts in following what God wants to do in their lives, which has touched so many others and inspired others to pursue intimacy with the living God. Thank you also for giving me a place to heal and find myself again.

Many thanks go out to my family, both through blood and through the spirit of Christ. We are one body in Jesus, and I could not have found the peace in my life that I have now without your wisdom and kind hearts.

Made in the USA
San Bernardino, CA
27 April 2014